Liguori Sacramental Preparation

Your Marriage
LEADER GUIDE

Deborah Meister

This *Leader Guide* provides an overview and practical procedures for leading engaged couples through the *Your Marriage* sacramental preparation program at the parish or diocesan level.

Imprimi Potest: Stephen T. Rehrauer, CSsR,
Provincial, Denver Province, the Redemptorists

Imprimatur: "In accordance with CIC 827, permission to publish has been granted on July 2, 2015, by the Most Reverend Edward M. Rice, Auxiliary Bishop, Archdiocese of St. Louis. Permission to publish is an indication that nothing contrary to Church teaching is contained in this work. It does not imply any endorsement of the opinions expressed in the publication; nor is any liability assumed by this permission."

Your Marriage Leader Guide published by Liguori Publications, Liguori, Missouri 63057.

To order, visit Liguori.org or call 800-325-9521.

Copyright © 2015 Liguori Publications

p ISBN 978-0-7648-2547-7

e ISBN 978-0-7648-7000-2

All Rights Reserved. No part of this publication may be reproduced, stored in a retrieval system, or transmitted in any form or by any means—electronic, mechanical, photocopy, recording, or any other—except for brief quotations in printed reviews, without the prior written permission of Liguori Publications.

Excerpts from *Vatican Council II: The Basic Sixteen Documents*, Revised Translation, copyright 1996 by Reverend Austin Flannery, OP; published by Costello Publishing Company, Inc., Northport, NY, are used by permission of the publisher. All Rights Reserved.

Excerpts from other Vatican documents are used with permission. Copyright *Libreria Editrice Vaticana* (© *Libreria Editrice Vaticana*)

Excerpts from English translation of the *Catechism of the Catholic Church* for the United States of America © 1994, United States Catholic Conference, Inc.—*Libreria Editrice Vaticana*; English translation of the *Catechism of the Catholic Church: Modifications from the Editio Typica* © 1997, United States Catholic Conference, Inc.—*Libreria Editrice Vaticana*.

Excerpts from the English translation of *Rite of Marriage* © 1969, International Commission on English in the Liturgy Corporation. All Rights Reserved. Used with permission.

Scripture texts in this work are taken from the *New American Bible*, revised edition © 2010, 1991, 1986, 1970 Confraternity of Christian Doctrine, Washington, D.C., and are used by permission of the copyright owner. All Rights Reserved. No part of the *New American Bible* may be reproduced in any form without permission in writing from the copyright owner.

Unless noted otherwise, images are from Shutterstock.

Liguori Publications, a nonprofit corporation, is an apostolate of the Redemptorists. To learn more about the Redemptorists, visit Redemptorists.com.

Printed in the United States of America
19 18 17 16 15 / 5 4 3 2 1
First Edition

About the author

Deborah Meister is an editor for Bayard, Inc., and an author with years of experience in education and parish ministry. Her former positions include editor for Liguori Publications and coordinator of family life for the Archdiocese of St. Louis, where she helped develop a comprehensive marriage-preparation program. She is a certified CRE/DRE and pastoral minister and holds master's degrees in theology and literature as well as a graduate certificate in pastoral care. She continues to serve parishes and publishers, especially in the realm of faith formation, spirituality and devotions, and catechesis. Her works have been published in a variety of print, audio, and digital media. Deborah Meister is married and the mother of two adult daughters.

Contents

About the Author 2

Before You Begin / Acknowledgments 5

Program Components 7
    The Essentials 7
    Qualities of an Effective Leader 8
    Materials and Supplies 9
    Preparing the Facility 10

Inside the Sessions 11
    Before the First Session 11
    At the First Session 12
    At Each Session 13
    Managing Time 14
    Breaks and Transitions 15
    Personal Narratives 16
    Determining Required Chapters 18

Program Schedules 19
    Four Sessions 19
    Two Full-day Sessions 20
    Six Sessions 21
    Weekend Retreat 22

Contents

Chapter Guides ... 23

- Opening and Closing Prayers ... 23
- Spirituality and Faith in Marriage ... 24
- Theology of Marriage ... 26
- Rite of Marriage ... 28
- Communication in Marriage ... 30
- Family of Origin ... 32
- Money and Marriage ... 34
- Intimacy ... 36
- Sexuality ... 38
- Natural Family Planning ... 40
- Children and Parenting ... 42
- Cohabitation ... 44
- Annulment and Convalidation ... 46
- Interchurch and Interfaith Marriages ... 48
- Military Marriage ... 50
- Closing Prayer Service ... 52

Maintaining an Effective Program ... 56

- Building Community ... 56
- Prayer for Marriage-preparation Leaders ... 57
- Evaluation Forms ... 58
- Resources ... 62

Before You Begin

The importance of your role as a marriage-preparation leader or sponsor cannot be overstated. This ministry needs you, and engaged couples need you, too. The Church emphasizes and values effective, meaningful sacramental preparation, and we are grateful for the indispensable role married couples play in this process.

Throughout history, marriage has come under fire from all sides: from questioning its necessity as an institution to challenging its very definition. Even when we agree on what marriage means, spouses face many challenges in keeping their relationship healthy, happy, and holy. That is why **marriage preparation is a shared, communal journey**—much more than just watching a few videos and answering some questions. As a facilitator, you represent not only your parish or diocese, but also the whole faith community in building a "culture of marriage" *(A Response to the Research,* USCCB Subcommittee on Marriage and Family Life, 2007).

Whether or not you have finally determined that God has called you to this ministry, begin here with a short prayer thanking God for directing you this far. As Jesus so often told his disciples, "Be not afraid." You are not alone. This *Leader Guide* and the *Participant Workbook* offer you a firm foundation on Catholic teaching as well as practical advice for the contemporary issues of daily life.

Acknowledgments

Your Marriage would not be possible without the diligent service of its publication and production teams. The wisdom, ministries, personal witnesses, and vocations of the workbook authors speak volumes that could not be contained in this program. On behalf of the parishes leading this program, we are ever grateful.

To the sacramental-preparation team at Liguori Publications—Angela Baumann, Mark Bernard, Julia DiSalvo, Chuck Healy, Gabriel Hernández, Joseph Snyder, and many other leaders, staff, and customers: Your hard work and feedback shed light on a great need in the Church and shaped a solution for a diverse community.

To the Salt River Production Group, in particular Chuck Neff and our video cast and crew, especially Fr. Byron Miller, CSsR: Thank you for the special and sacred presence you bring to Catholic couples everywhere.

Program Components

The Essentials

Every parish is responsible for offering marriage preparation according to the direction of the local ordinary. The *Your Marriage* program meets the U.S. Conference of Catholic Bishops' recommendations for preparing couples who seek the sacrament and provides the materials and training you need to facilitate this ministry as modeled in the ***National Pastoral Initiative for Marriage*** (USCCB, 2005).

What is Catholic marriage preparation?

Most couples will attend a series of sessions or a retreat and often meet separately with the priest or deacon who will witness their vows. The sessions include instruction in what the Catholic faith teaches about marriage and touches on the essentials of Christian living. It also brings the couple into a conversation about their current needs and challenges in the context of their faith(s) and assists the parish in determining their capacity for entering freely into marriage as directed in the *Code of Canon Law*.

How long does it last?

The length of time spent in preparation varies by diocese, though most ask the couples to meet with a priest or deacon before setting the wedding date and allow for a minimum of six months for preparation.

What's in *Your Marriage*?

The *Participant Workbook* **presents the core program material**, from the nature and purpose of marriage to practical suggestions and guided practice in relationship skills. **Each chapter covers an essential topic**, applies it using various activities, and ends with reflection and discussion questions. Leaders introduce these topics and serve as living examples of the values and teachings therein. *In this guide, as a visual aid, italic type will denote workbook pages.*

The *Program DVD*'s video segments complement and highlight each chapter, feature testimonies from Catholic spouses, and stimulate the couples' conversations. With little to no exception, **both the bride and the groom will attend every session and complete the material together.** For long-distance relationships, this may present a challenge. Your diocese may have separate guidelines for these couples, especially for those in the military. The *Your Marriage* workbook and video can be used in these circumstances with prior approval.

Finally, **Liguori Publications provides a variety of resources** for those who want more on the theology of marriage, Catholic teaching, communication, and other relevant topics. For online material, references, and links, visit *Liguori.org/marriage*.

Program Components

Qualities of an Effective Leader

Marriage preparation's purposes are to form couples in the specific vocation of marriage and provide them with catechesis and spiritual aids for growing in their faith together.

The experiences of the facilitating couple(s) are instrumental in fulfilling these goals along with the program material. Leaders do not teach or lecture. **Rather, they share their own stories of faith and marriage** and offer a personal invitation to the vocation from the Church. As guides and models, they help engaged couples better understand and personally desire:

- the care and love of the Church for their marriage.
- God's unconditional love present in the covenant.
- deep communication between spouses and with God.
- authentic discovery and intimate knowledge of one another.
- the holiness in sexuality and procreation.
- that through marriage they will bear witness to God's love.
- an increased faith and friendship with Jesus.
- living for one another and not selfishly.
- a lifelong commitment to the wedding vows.

Effective leaders have certain qualities that enable them to better journey with the couples. Pastors and leaders should review this list to determine who possesses them and develop those they lack:

- Interested in supporting a "culture of marriage"
- Respectful of others' experiences, thoughts, and concerns
- Strong listener; attempts to understand the other;
- Consistent in valuing hospitality and discretion;
- Open to questions without judging;
- Humble in stating knowledge (or lack thereof);
- Comfortable with being challenged;
- Willing to share their faith, feelings, successes, and failures;
- Well-prepared, organized, and able to keep a group on schedule;
- Flexible in nature; avoids controlling.

One individual may not possess every desired quality, yet a married couple has twice the potential. *Many* can be good leaders as they are, and over time, we *all* can develop these traits if we are so motivated. Help your parish and team develop these qualities through basic training or in separate enrichment workshops for all your ministries.

Program Components

Materials and Supplies

Every couple attending *Your Marriage* needs to have two workbooks: one for the woman and one for the man. This allows each of them to read the chapters ahead of the sessions and write down responses to the activities, questions, and evaluation independently. **Leaders also will need their own copies of the workbook.** Besides being an essential resource, many enjoy the ease of reference and benefit from reviewing and marking the material throughout—not just at the start of—their ministry.

For every session, have on hand:

- A private, prayerful setting;
- Individual copies of *Your Marriage: Participant Workbook;*
- Copies of *Your Marriage: Leader Guide* for each facilitator and presider;
- One copy of *Your Marriage: Program DVD;*
- Compatible disk player and screen and sound equipment for presenting the video segments;
- Notebooks or paper, and pens;
- Chairs for participants, and tables for medium and large groups;
- Bibles (*NABRE* recommended);
- Refreshments;
- Name tags;
- Icebreaker material(s), as needed;
- Personal narratives, well-crafted and succinct;
- Handouts, as needed (Additional resources are available at *Liguori.org/marriage*.);
- *Optional:* Device for playing quiet background music during private times.

For the last session, have on hand:

- Copies of the *Your Marriage* Certificate and/or official letter signifying completion of the program for each couple (available at *Liguori.org/marriage*);
- Stationery and envelopes or copies of the first-anniversary "Love Letters" activity for each couple for the Closing Prayer Service (see page 55 and online);
- Individual copies of the evaluation forms (see pages 58–61 and online).

Program Components

Preparing the Facility

Couples should feel welcome from the moment they arrive. Although some consider marriage preparation to be "jumping through hoops," usually they have come voluntarily and without impediments to taking their vows. **Let them know right away that they are welcome** by giving clear directions to the room and setting up a table with name tags, supplies, and refreshments.

Your location may be predetermined or even reserved for you, or you may be responsible for obtaining a space on your own. Meeting in a home lends a friendly and intimate atmosphere, but any space can become warmer and less institutional. Before the couples arrive, make sure the seating is sufficient and the room is clear of any clutter or remains of the last event. If possible, add a touch of flowers or candy at each table.

> *– Tip –*
> If the location isn't sized well, the music and seating can be adjusted to increase its effectiveness.

The best locations offer a quiet space with enough room to spread out and create a sense of comfort and privacy. When laying out furniture and equipment, consider:

- viewing angles for presentations, group sharing, and watching the video;
- space for each couple to privately discuss the activities and reflection questions;
- traffic flow between the main group area and other spaces, especially for those with mobility needs;
- accessibility of electrical outlets, additional supplies, and personal belongings.

Inside the Sessions

Before the First Session

Whether your sessions are prescheduled, preformatted, or arranged according to mutual availability, obey the instructions given by your parish or diocese. As you become more experienced and familiar with your particular program, you can more easily adapt it to meet your needs.

1. **Gather a list of the brides' and grooms' names,** contact information, and their parishes or faith communities. (This can double as a check-in list.)

2. **Contact every registered couple in advance** to introduce yourself, remind them of the time, place, and required materials, and answer any questions. (One call, either to the bride or the groom, is sufficient.) If they have not received their workbooks at this point, direct them to the proper office, staff member, or marketplace.

3. **Begin to build expectations.** Convey the importance of reading the initial chapter text(s) prior to the first session. Assure them that all that is needed is a general understanding; you will discuss the key points, answer questions, and complete some activities in each session.

4. **Begin to build a rapport.** The relationship between couples and their sponsors provides familiarity and extends beyond the program and into the parish community.

Group Dynamics

As the number of sessions can vary, so can the number of people meeting and facilitating with you. The dynamics will change, depending on the personalities and size of the group. Generally, leaders can "set the tone." Couples do not need to share with the group as much as with their future spouse. While facilitators are there to ease, and to some extent certify, this process, the critical sharing goes on whenever the couple discusses the topics.

This guide identifies three common group sizes:

- LARGE—ten to twenty couples, with one to three married, facilitating couples;

- SMALL—three to six couples, with one or two married, facilitating couples;

- INDIVIDUAL—one or two couples with one married, facilitating couple.

Inside the Sessions

At the First Session

1. **Welcome the couples and introduce yourselves** (how long you've been married, number of children, your parish). Make a special point of welcoming non-Catholics and explain that, while the content reflects Church teaching, they will find common and familiar ground in every chapter.

2. **Break the ice early** with a brief activity. The couples may introduce themselves to the group or just to their table. Varying tables between sessions generates fuller group unity, diversity in discussions, and avoids competition or cliques.

3. **State your expectations,** give directions to the restrooms, and offer any instructions or announcements. Emphasize that time is limited, and request that attendees return from discussions or breaks when they are called. **Their conversations here are only the beginning,** and meaningful interactions should continue through and beyond the wedding. Also remind them that you and their presider are available outside of the sessions for further guidance and support.

4. **Mention confidentiality.** Marriage preparation involves sensitive topics and personal, often private, information. While most details will remain between the spouses, make it clear that what is shared in the room stays in the room.

Icebreaker Ideas

- Ask each couple to share how long they have known one another and give a simple prize (candy, small prayer booklet) for the shortest or longest time. Or use the nearest wedding date or the wedding date closest to your own anniversary.

- If the couples are seated at tables, consider totaling the number of wedding party members or length of time before the weddings collectively. This light conversation creates a friendly atmosphere.

– Tip –

Full- or half-day sessions normally include a snack, refreshments, and/or a light meal. Knowing and meeting people's basic needs will help them to relax, focus their attention, and lower any resistance to participating.

Inside the Sessions

At Each Session

1. **Start with Scripture and a prayer.** Have one leader proclaim a reading from the Rite of Marriage and another read a prayer, alternating or taking turns if desired. Do not rush; leave time for silence and reflection. An opening and closing prayer can be found on page 23 of this *Leader Guide*, page 5 of the *Participant Workbook*, and at *Liguori.org/marriage*.

2. **List the chapters covered.** Early on, remind the couples which topics you will cover. Before dismissing them, answer any important or lingering questions and review their reading and activity responsibilities. Reading prior to the sessions will help them form questions and improve their discussions and time spent as a group.

3. **End well and on time.** Try to find a natural closing point that leaves a few minutes for tidying, gathering personal items, and goodbyes. Don't dismiss the couples before sharing a prayer.

> **– Tip –**
>
> These four readings from the Rite of Marriage are suggested. A full list is in the *Participant Workbook*'s "Wedding Ceremony Planner" *(workbook pages 52–53)*. Read the passages from a Bible or study *Lectionary*, since they're God's divine and inspired word.
>
> - Matthew 7:21, 24–29
> - John 15:9–12
> - Mark 10:6–9
> - Matthew 5:13–16

Inside the Sessions

Managing Time

Before the first session, most couples have already spent hours talking about and planning for their wedding. The time they spend on this program will pale in comparison. Facilitators must be ready to **keep the group on schedule in order to adequately cover every topic**. Moreover, the bride and groom need to have sufficient time in each session to talk to one another about the material.

A well-planned session may get off track after someone asks a tough question.

Always respect the questions and give as complete a response as time allows. If you are unsure of how to answer or of relevant Church teachings:

- direct the person to an appropriate office or contact;
- check recommended resources and trusted sources;
- meet privately with the couple to answer questions more thoroughly;
- promise to have an answer at the next session.

— *Tip* —

Every couple meets with a priest or deacon during marriage preparation, and they will be able to ask him questions. Never pretend to know more than you actually do or give incomplete or misleading information for the sake of a response.

Inside the Sessions

Breaks and Transitions

As leaders become proficient in moving couples through the material, they will be better able to judge when to spend more or less time on each topic. Leaders must be aware of the time in order to avoid rushing the group or skipping entire sections. **Rather than curb a reflection, discussion, or activity, leave out a break or personal narrative.** Try to respect those couples who may have long drives, early mornings, or other commitments. Be prepared to gently end discussions or bring the group back together after breaks in a timely fashion. Encourage each couple to continue discussing what they have discovered on their own.

All groups eventually need a break, and without an eye on the clock these breaks will wreak havoc on the schedule.

1. **Set strict break lengths.** The program schedules allow at least fifteen minutes per session, which can be broken into several shorter breaks if preferred. Five minutes for the restroom and ten for snacks are sufficient. If a full meal is involved, give at least thirty minutes for plating and cleanup.

2. **Remind the couples to move around.** Invite them to stand up, stretch, use the restroom, and meet and greet the others. Some may prefer to stay seated and continue talking. Either way, when a room has just enough chairs for each person, it is easier to tell when everyone has returned.

3. **Give a thirty-second warning.** Find a reasonable means of bringing people back that considers their need to wrap up conversations and shift their attention.

4. **Move them into the next topic.** When the time is up, promptly resume with a transitional statement, question, or activity that engages the group with the next section or topic. **Time for questions should be provided at some point in each session.**

– Tip –

Everyone wants to end on time, but no one wants to leave knowing the material hasn't been covered fully. *Beginning on time* is the first step.

Inside the Sessions

Personal Narratives

Leaders will share personal stories during each session. **Depending on their length and relevance, more than one per topic can be shared;** for example, a woman and man may both have stories to share about overcoming obstacles in communication.

Not everyone has a gift for storytelling, but we all have good stories to tell. Focus on improving your narratives by:

- preparing each one carefully, keeping it brief and to the point;
- ensuring each story has a purpose and stresses an important matter of faith or practical matter of the marital relationship; (Most will likely contain elements of both.)
- ensuring the purpose is not lost in the details, stray sections, or poorly chosen remarks;
- practicing each one aloud (maybe in front of your spouse).

Your narratives may be humorous or sentimental, but their purpose is not to entertain, pass the time, or showcase the "days of our lives." **The stories must remain relevant to the material and deliver a message that benefits the audience.** Leaders share their experiences in order to further the couples' understanding of the topic, its application(s) to their relationship, and of each other.

– Tip –

To create a personal narrative with a clear purpose, ask yourself:

1. Why am I telling this story? What does it convey?

2. What are the two most important points that I want to illustrate? (Avoid generalities.)

3. How do these points relate directly to the topic at hand? (The couples should be able to easily apply your story to the presented material.)

Choose stories that have one or two unifying themes such as forgiveness, working through communication gaps, and financial struggles that strengthened the marriage. When you tie the stories together with common threads, each story builds on the last without having to introduce an entirely new scenario. Of course, the idea of carrying one theme over several narratives may sound daunting. Over time, as you hone your skills, this will become second nature.

Every new session and group of engaged couples offers you an opportunity to reflect on your marriage, events that improved your relationship, and times when you learned a valuable lesson. All relationships change over time, for better and for worse. Moreover, our relationships frequently influence how we live out our faith and relationship with God.

Your parish or diocese may invite you to a workshop or mention resources you can review on your own. Take advantage of any learning opportunities, no matter how skilled you are at public speaking.

— **Tip** —

Looking over the chapter's activities and reflection questions may give you ideas for sharing pertinent experiences that segue smoothly from the review. The narratives you choose will change over time and can help you to remain passionate about the subject matter.

— **Tip** —

Parishes and dioceses encourage facilitators to improve their presentation skills and knowledge by providing or supporting guided training in sacramental preparation, faith formation, catechesis, and evangelization. Most leaders, whether lay sponsors or professional ministers, enjoy meeting each another and sharing their experiences and best practices. A Mass and dinner for your leaders go a long way in showing appreciation for all they do.

Inside the Sessions

Determining Required Chapters

Each parish or diocese is charged with determining each couple's sacramental status and readiness. To achieve these goals, *Your Marriage* recommends that **every couple complete the first ten chapters of the workbook**. The final four chapters have been included to meet particular needs and are not considered applicable to every couple. However, **they should be assigned and considered mandatory whenever relevant** to the couple's situation. In groups where most or all couples would benefit, incorporating these chapters into the main program is the best option. When additional steps or social sensitivities warrant private or extra meetings, leaders should communicate this stipulation to couples well in advance and schedule accordingly.

1. **Cohabitation**—especially for couples living together, though the schedules below always include this chapter, since the themes benefit all couples.

2. **Annulment and Convalidation**—for previously or currently married couples. Annulment assumes a civil divorce, and convalidation assumes a civil wedding. The priest or pastor can assist you in determining the couple's sacramental status, as it affects the marriage-preparation process.

3. **Interchurch and Interfaith Marriages**—for couples in which one partner is not Catholic. This chapter assumes at least one partner is an active, confirmed Catholic.

4. **Military Marriage**—for couples in which one or both partners are actively commissioned in a branch of the armed forces or military reserves. This chapter may also benefit civilian couples who work on base, closely with the military, or face lengthy separation due to professional travel or incarceration.

Program Schedules

Four Sessions (three hours each)

First Session: What Is Marriage?

Welcome / Hospitality	15 minutes
Spirituality and Faith in Marriage	50 minutes
Break	15 minutes
Theology of Marriage	50 minutes
Rite of Marriage	25–50 minutes, depending on annulment
Annulment and Convalidation	if applicable, 25 minutes

Second Session: Love and Relationship

Welcome / Hospitality	15 minutes
Communication in Marriage	50 minutes
Family of Origin	25–50 minutes, depending on intermarriage
Break	15 minutes
Intimacy	50 minutes
Interchurch and Interfaith Marriages	if applicable, 25 minutes

Third Session: Sex and Marriage

Welcome / Hospitality	15 minutes
Sexuality	50 minutes
Natural Family Planning	50 minutes
Break	15 minutes
Cohabitation	25–50 minutes, depending on follow-up/review needs

Fourth Session: Family Matters

Welcome / Hospitality	15 minutes
Money and Marriage	50 minutes
Break	15 minutes
Children and Parenting	50 minutes
Military Marriage	if applicable, 25 minutes
Final Review*	25 minutes, depending on military
Closing Prayer Service	25 minutes

*Use this time to answer any last questions, complete an additional activity, complete the evaluation form, and/or discuss wedding arrangements.

Program Schedules

Two Full-day Sessions (six hours each)

First Session: The Marriage Relationship

Welcome / Hospitality	15 minutes
Spirituality and Faith in Marriage	50 minutes
Annulment and Convalidation	if applicable, 20 minutes
Theology of Marriage	50 minutes
Rite of Marriage	25 minutes
Break / Meal	40 minutes
Communication in Marriage	50 minutes
Money and Marriage	50 minutes
Break	20 minutes
Intimacy	40 minutes

*If annulment or convalidation do not apply, the extra time can be divided among the Intimacy, Money, and/or Communication chapters, especially the activities, or used to answer additional questions or discuss wedding arrangements.

Second Session: Children and Family

Welcome / Hospitality	20 minutes
Family of Origin	50 minutes
Sexuality	50 minutes
Cohabitation	25–50 minutes
Break / Meal	40 minutes
Natural Family Planning	50 minutes
Children and Parenting	50 minutes
Interchurch and Interfaith Marriages	if applicable, 25–40 minutes
Military Marriage	if applicable, 25–40 minutes
Closing Prayer Service	30 minutes

† *With no additional chapters, devote 50 minutes to Cohabitation and use the extra 20 minutes to review, answer any last questions, and complete the evaluation form.*

† *With one additional chapter, devote 40 minutes to that topic and 25 minutes to Cohabitation. Five minutes remain.*

† *With two additional chapters, devote 25 minutes to each of the three chapters. Five minutes will need to be shaved from the total session time.*

* *Each session allows 15 to 20 minutes for welcome/hospitality and other needs.*

Program Schedules

Six Sessions (two hours each)

First Session: Laying the Foundation

Spirituality and Faith in Marriage	50 minutes
Cohabitation	25–50 minutes, dep. on addl. chapters
Annulment and Convalidation	if applicable, 25 minutes
Interchurch and Interfaith Marriages	if applicable, 25 minutes
Military Marriage	if applicable, 25 minutes

† *With no additional chapters, allow 50 minutes for Cohabitation.*

† *With one additional chapter, allow 25 minutes for that topic and Cohabitation.*

† *With two additional chapters, allow 25 minutes for each of those chapters, and move Cohabitation to the Fifth Session (25 minutes).*

† *With three additional chapters, move Cohabitation as above and one additional chapter to the Second Session (25 minutes).*

Second Session: God's Plan for Marriage

Theology of Marriage	50 minutes
Rite of Marriage	25–50 minutes, dep. on First Session

Third Session: Building Unity

Communication in Marriage	50 minutes
Intimacy	50 minutes

Fourth Session: Day by Day

Family of Origin	50 minutes
Money and Marriage	50 minutes

Fifth Session: Coming Together

Sexuality	50 minutes
Natural Family Planning	25–50 minutes, dep. on Cohabitation

Sixth Session: Children and Family

Children and Parenting	50 minutes
Final Review*	25 minutes
Closing Prayer Service	25 minutes

*Use this time to answer any last questions, complete an additional activity, complete the evaluation form, and/or discuss wedding arrangements.

Program Schedules

Weekend Retreat

Timing is based on the six-session format, with a suggested Friday–Sunday schedule.

Friday Evening

6:30	Welcome / Hospitality
7:00	**Laying the Foundation** (see "First Session")
8:45	Free time (fellowship)

Saturday Morning

8:00	Breakfast
8:30	**God's Plan for Marriage** (see "Second Session")
10:15	Break / Snack
10:30	**Building Unity** (see "Third Session")

Saturday Afternoon

12:15	Lunch
1:00	**Day by Day** (see "Fourth Session")
2:45	Break (with optional Sacrament of Reconciliation)
3:15	**Coming Together** (see "Fifth Session")

Saturday Evening

5:00	Dinner
5:45	**Children and Family** (see "Sixth Session")
7:30	Final Review and Evaluation Forms
8:00	Closing Prayer Service / Presentation of Certificates
8:30	Free Time (packing)

Sunday Morning

8:00	Mass
8:30	Breakfast
9:00	Dismissal

Chapter Guides

Opening and Closing Prayers

Opening Prayer

Loving God, you have called us here this day
 to prepare as best we can for the Sacrament of Matrimony.
Bless us with the grace we need to open our hearts and minds
 to the holy mystery of marriage.
We desire to live as man and wife with a love that never fails.
Bless our conversations and our quiet moments with your wisdom.
We rely on the foundation of faith and prayer in building a strong marriage.
Bless our love with the grace to be forgiving and unselfish.
We desire to let our marriage shine with the love and light of Christ
 to be a sign of your unconditional and everlasting love for the whole world.

Amen.

Closing Prayer

O God, your love and compassion speak to us through one another.
You have called us here (today/tonight) to reflect on and understand better
 the lifelong covenant with one another in marriage.
Help us to be open to the grace we need to prepare well, to truly discern our vows,
 and to prepare ourselves to build a strong marriage.
Thank you for your presence as we continue to share all that we have received
 and grow in love and unity.
Bless our conversations and help us to see your face in one another.

Amen.

Chapter Guides

Spirituality and Faith in Marriage *(50 minutes)*

Welcome and Hospitality

Greet the couples as they arrive or return. Be sure they have the required materials, and provide supplies as needed. Begin on time.

 ### Key Points (2 minutes)

Say, "First we will discuss spirituality in the context of marriage. This topic teaches us that…"

1. *Christ is the foundation of the domestic church.* This connection is described on *workbook page 14.*
2. *Faith within marriage can be challenging.* This chapter addresses some common challenges, including different religious practices (*workbook page 11*).
3. *How to share a life of prayer.* Suggestions for and benefits to praying together are found on *workbook page 12.*

Transition to the videos with a question. Take responses and reactions after the segment concludes.

What do you value about your spirituality and faith? What do you find difficult?

 ### Videos (7 minutes)

Play the "Introduction" and "Spirituality and Faith in Marriage" segments.

 ### Review (10 minutes)

- Describe in your own words a solid foundation for a strong marriage.
- Explain that loving someone is a choice, and marriage is a decision to love—freely, completely, and continually.
- Ask the couples for examples of prayer. Affirm their answers. When we pray, we are called to listen to God as well as speak. Ask them to envision praying together. Shared prayer requires vulnerability, trust, and humility. It is a form of intimate contact and one of the best ways to build a loving relationship with each other.

The *Catechism of the Catholic Church* offers insights into the meaning, necessity, and models of prayer (see *CCC* 2559–2745).

Chapter Guides

 **Personal Narrative (5 minutes)**

Using a specific personal experience, illustrate one or two key points to help the couples understand and respond to the content.

- How did you approach the spiritual side of your marriage?
- How has your religious practice changed (or not) over the years?
- What feelings and challenges did you discover in praying and living out your faith together?
- How did you resolve any conflicts that arose? Connect "the Benefits of Praying Together" on *workbook page 12* to your experience.

 **Activity (10 minutes)**

Have each couple choose one activity that most interests them and thoughtfully consider and write down their responses before sharing with their fiancé(e). Instruct the couples to complete the remaining activities prior to their wedding in order to complete their preparation.

"Scripture Support," *workbook page 9.*

"Different Religious Practices," *page 11* (see key point 2).

"Determining a Common Prayer Style," *page 13* (see key point 3).

 **Reflection Questions (16 minutes)**

Workbook page 16:

After each individual considers and writes his or her responses, the couple will discuss them privately. Encourage them to do more than read what they wrote. They should help one another understand their beliefs and feelings. Going in order and racing through every question is not as important as starting some real conversations that will continue and deepen over time.

25

Chapter Guides

Theology of Marriage (50 minutes)

Welcome and Hospitality

Greet the couples as they arrive or return. Be sure they have the required materials, and provide supplies as needed. Begin on time.

 ## Key Points (2 minutes)

Say, "Now we will discuss the theology of marriage. This topic answers these questions:"

1. *What makes marriage unique?* Three ways are listed on *workbook page 22*.
2. *What are the "goods" of marriage?* The workbook explains the three goods on *pages 25–29*.
3. *What is meant by "natural law?"* This concept is defined and supported on *workbook pages 32–33*.

Transition to the video with a question. Take responses and reactions after the segment concludes.

What gifts or benefits do you expect to receive in marriage? How do these things reflect the teachings of Christ?

 ## Video (6 minutes)

Play the "Theology of Marriage" segment.

 ## Review (12 minutes)

- Turn to "What Makes a Marriage Special" (see page 27 and *workbook page 22*). Give an example or two, then ask the couples for more.

- Assess their understanding of "proper" and "natural" by differentiating between what is "natural" and what is meant by the Church's term "natural law." You may need to consult supplemental resources for clear examples.

- Emphasize the great value and necessity of the three "goods": openness to procreation, fidelity, and an unbreakable covenant (*workbook pages 25–29*). Remind them that they will consent to these realities on their wedding day.

 ## Personal Narrative (5 minutes)

Using a specific personal experience, illustrate one or two key points to help the couples understand and respond to the content.

- Give an example or two of how the "goods" are manifested and have value in your marriage.

- Share how you have experienced and benefitted from the grace of the sacrament and God's presence in your marriage.

Chapter Guides

 **Activities (10 minutes)**

Introduce "What Makes Marriage Special?" and define the terms below to provide clarity and context. Have the couples thoughtfully consider and write down their responses before sharing with their fiancé(e). If time permits, move on to "Rising Above." Regardless, instruct them to complete the remaining activities prior to their wedding in order to complete their preparation.

"What Makes Marriage Special?" *workbook pages 22–24,* key point 1: Define these terms for the couples:
Exclusive: Only one such relationship occurring, at least at any given time (such as sexual monogamy).
Supreme: The highest value and priority is given to this relationship.
Reproductive potential: The partners have the biological ability to conceive children with each other. This is a matter of physical gender, not fertility, and doesn't factor in adoption or surrogacy.

"Theology in Action," *page 27:* First ask for responses to two or three of the selected verses, and follow with a few minutes for couples to discuss the remainder privately.

"Rising Above," *pages 30–31:* Completing the charts with the couples will help them understand the three "goods" and integrate the "natural law" into their views on marriage (see key point 2).

For each chart, prompt the couples for biological and human/social examples. Then provide the spiritual examples and purposes below:

Washing: Example: Baptism; *Purposes:* "Bath of rebirth and renewal" (Titus 3:5) and forgiveness / removal of sin (*CCC* 405, 1263)

Art: Examples: sacred art and religious icons; *Purposes:* "evoking and glorifying…the transcendent mystery of God" (*CCC* 2502, see also *Sacrosanctum Concilium*, 122)

 **Reflection Questions (15 minutes)**
Workbook page 34:

After each individual considers and writes his or her responses, the couple will discuss them privately. Encourage them to do more than read what they wrote. They should help one another understand their beliefs and feelings. Going in order and racing through every question is not as important as starting some real conversations that will continue and deepen over time.

27

Chapter Guides

Rite of Marriage (25 minutes / 50 minutes)

Welcome and Hospitality

Greet the couples as they arrive or return. Be sure they have the required materials, and provide supplies as needed. *A Bible will be needed for some of the activities in this chapter.* Begin on time.

 ### Key Points (2 minutes)

Say, "Now let's discuss the rite of marriage—the wedding ceremony. This chapter teaches us that…"

1. *Marriage is effected through the exchange of consent.* The four steps to this declaration are listed on *workbook page 44.*
2. *As a sacrament, the Rite of Marriage is often celebrated within the Mass* (see *workbook page 40*).
3. *Within the rite, there are opportunities to personalize the ceremony.* The Wedding Ceremony Planner starts on *workbook page 48* and lists many of these options.

Transition to the video with a question. Take responses and reactions after the segment concludes.

How do you envision your wedding ceremony? Do you have a favorite word or phrase from the wedding vows?

 ### Video (5 minutes)

Play the "Rite of Marriage" segment.

 ### Review (8 or 13 minutes)

- Remind couples that the Mass is the highest representation of what marriage should also reflect: God's eternal, unconditional, and self-giving love.

- Explain the necessity of giving free and full consent. Use negative examples to illustrate constraints or pressures to marry (for example, mental health, joint ownership of property, unplanned pregnancy).

- Marriage preparation is the time and place for each individual to fully and finally discern whether entering into marriage with his or her fiancé(e) is appropriate. Encourage couples in this necessary process by providing time and space for private reflection in the sessions. The Cohabitation chapter's video segment and activities also address this discernment (see pages 44–45 and *workbook page 186*).

Assist the couples in tracking down any necessary documents such as baptismal records. A list of diocesan contacts and what is required in your area is very helpful.

Chapter Guides

 **Personal Narrative (5 minutes)**

Using a specific personal experience, illustrate one or two key points to help the couples understand and respond to the content.

- Reflect on your selection of readings for your wedding and share the personal relevance of those passages.
- Avoid telling stories about planning your wedding or the wedding day that do not have instructive purposes. Consider sharing details that offer opportunities for meaningful interaction and discussion in your families.

 **Activities (5 or 10 minutes)**

Introduce "Reflect on a Wedding Reading" and direct the couples to the list of passages in the Wedding Ceremony Planner (*workbook pages 52–53*). If time permits, begin "Pray for Us." Encourage them to complete the remaining activities as soon as possible, as they assist them in planning their wedding liturgy.

"Reflect on a Wedding Reading," *workbook pages 43, 52–53:* The personal narrative on your own selection of readings may guide them in this exercise.

"Pray for Us," *page 46:* Choose one example to demonstrate how to enlarge the target and give them a few minutes to write one petition. Ask if anyone would like to share it with the group.

"Wedding Ceremony Planner," *page 48:* This will be completed gradually and in coordination with their presider. Couples can download and print a separate copy of these pages at *Liguori.org/marriage*.

 **Reflection Questions (15 minutes, depending)**

Workbook page 56:

After each individual considers and writes his or her responses, the couple will discuss them privately. Encourage them to do more than read what they wrote. They should help one another understand their beliefs and feelings. Going in order and racing through every question is not as important as starting some real conversations that will continue and deepen over time.

Chapter Guides

Communication in Marriage (50 minutes)

Welcome and Hospitality

Greet the couples as they arrive or return. Be sure they have the required materials, and provide supplies as needed.

Consider providing a separate time for receiving the sacrament of reconciliation, which is available to all baptized Christians. Begin on time.

 ## Key Points (2 minutes)

Say, "Now we will discuss communication in marriage. This topic teaches us that…"

1. *Communication is understanding, not just an expression* (see workbook page 62).
2. *Communication is a skill and can be learned.* The activities in this chapter provide guided practice in this skill.
3. *Always seek and speak the truth.* Workbook pages 65–66 walk couples through the steps of this process.

Transition to the video with a question. Take responses and reactions after the segment concludes.

What is an example of your typical body language?

 ## Video (6 minutes)

Play the "Communication in Marriage" segment.

 ## Review (10 minutes)

- Communication can (and should) be improved with practice. It is directed toward understanding, healing, and humility. For example, a genuine apology is an expression of love.

- Listening is often more important than talking. A good listener does not think about a perfect response while the other person is still speaking but pays careful attention to what is being said and how the speaker is feeling (see also *workbook page 68*).

- Honesty and respect for your spouse's view will aid in productive discussions, as will taking time to make sure your words are accurate and constructive. When discerning what matters to discuss and when, the *Catechism* has a wealth of guidance. Consider the relevance of:

  + Sincerity, candor, and secrets in light of the Eighth Commandment (*CCC* 2464–2499);

  + Scandal in light of the Fifth Commandment (*CCC* 2284–2287);

  + The virtues of prudence and temperance (*CCC* 1806, 1808), which are related to restraint and discretion.

 **Personal Narrative (5 minutes)**

Using a specific personal experience, illustrate one or two key points to help the couples understand and respond to the content.

- Share the communication skills you brought to your marriage and those you lack(ed).
- Illustrate a communication disaster and what it taught you about communicating with your spouse.
- How do you communicate differently today than when you were first married?

 **Activities (10 minutes)**

Introduce "Now You Try It!" **and model the steps** using a complaint one of you has had about the other. If time permits, introduce "He Said/She Said" and offer some *positive* statements and affirmations to balance out the *negative* examples. Instruct the couples to complete the remaining activities prior to the wedding in order to complete their preparation.

"He Said/She Said," *workbook page 62*

"Now You Try It!" *page 66*

"Forgiveness and Reconciliation," *workbook page 69:*

✢ To help couples witness the importance of vulnerability and honesty, model numbers 2 and 3 of this activity aloud (asking your spouse for forgiveness for a specific infringement and offering amends).

✢ If time is dedicated for the Examination of Conscience, play soft music to enhance privacy and reflection. Provide paper and pen for note-takers and tissues, too. If the Sacrament of Reconciliation isn't immediately available, encourage the couples to attend as soon as possible. They should travel as a couple and pray together before and/or afterward.

 **Reflection Questions (17 minutes)**
Workbook page 70:

After each individual considers and writes his or her responses, the couple will discuss them privately. Encourage them to do more than read what they wrote. They should help one another understand their beliefs and feelings. Going in order and racing through every question is not as important as starting some real conversations that will continue and deepen over time.

Family of Origin (25 minutes / 50 minutes)

Welcome and Hospitality

Greet the couples as they arrive or return. Be sure they have the required materials. Provide supplies as needed. Begin on time.

 ## Key Points (2 minutes)

Say, "Now let's talk about our families of origin. This chapter teaches us about…"

1. *Harmonizing differences while strengthening new connections. Workbook page 75* lists healthy connections to strengthen.
2. *The four temperaments.* Each one is detailed on *workbook pages 80–83*.
3. *Becoming our best selves together* (see activity on *workbook page 84*).

Transition to the video with a question. Take responses and reactions after the segment concludes.

Reflect on your current roles and relationships. Are you a sibling, friend, colleague, student, parent, disciple?

 ## Video (5 minutes)

Play the "Family of Origin" segment.

 ## Review (5 or 8 minutes)

- Understanding who we are and why we react in certain ways can make a significant impact on your marriage.
- Do not presume your spouse will change learned habits. Be patient; this takes commitment and attention from both the husband and wife.
- While we are called to give ourselves to God and our spouse fully, this doesn't mean we have to be perfect. Self-improvement in a marriage involves forgiveness and helping one another reach shared goals.

 ## Personal Narrative (5 minutes)

Using a specific personal experience, illustrate one or two key points to help the couples understand and respond to the content.

- Give an example of when you or your spouse realized your family traditions were different. How did you each react? What ultimately resulted?
- Describe how you and your spouse have built your own traditions out of the blessings and challenges of your respective families of origin.
- Choose a category from the "Becoming Our Best Self" exercise *(workbook page 84)* and describe how you and your spouse are working together to achieve your target(s).

Chapter Guides

 **Activities (8 or 15 minutes)**

Introduce "What Would You Do?" and brainstorm some solutions as a group. If time permits, introduce "Becoming Our Best Self" and share some of your personal targets. Instruct the couples to complete the remaining activities prior to the wedding in order to complete their preparation.

"What Would You Do?" *workbook pages 76–77:* Responses will vary, and couples should be able to explain their reasoning. Suggested answers are below:

1. **Sean's wife must be honest and vulnerable** in sharing how she feels. Sean needs to understand the effects of his words and should consider new ways of sharing.

2. **Isabella's husband should explain** the confusion her tone creates and ask for clarity, especially in important matters. Together they can practice sincerity and express appreciation for the gifts of honesty and strong communication.

3. **Both partners should seek consensus and reconciliation.** They can begin by apologizing and forgiving each other. Chris will need to practice humility and patience and seek out Emily's approval more. Emily needs to respect and consider Chris' input when making decisions.

4. **Jamie can pause before she speaks.** Counting, breathing, saying a short prayer, or slowing down will create a calmer response. Also, she could write down her response first or take a break when a topic gets too hot.

5. **David needs to understand** the difference between diligence and perfectionism. David should be reminded of our inherent dignity and ongoing efforts and successes. David can practice patience and mercy, allowing us to improve at God's pace and take on challenges and healthy risks.

"Temperament Chart," *pages 82–83,* key point 2

"Becoming Our Best Self," *page 84,* key point 3:
If modeling this activity, prepare some targets ahead of time. Have couples begin with physical and spiritual; the others are easier done on their own.

 **Reflection Questions (15 minutes, depending)**

Workbook page 86:

After each individual writes his or her responses, the couple will discuss them privately. They should help one another understand their beliefs and feelings and begin some real conversations that will continue and deepen over time.

33

Chapter Guides

Money and Marriage (50 minutes)

Welcome and Hospitality

Greet the couples as they arrive or return. Be sure they have the required materials, and provide supplies as needed. Begin on time.

 ## Key Points (2 minutes)

Say, "Now we will discuss money in the context of marriage. This topic teaches us that…"

1. *Stewardship and generosity connect your faith and finances.* These topics are discussed on *workbook page 93*.
2. *Create a shared budget and financial plan.* The tools and activities in this chapter help the couples accomplish this task.
3. *Savings and wealth creation are necessary* (see *workbook pages 100 and 104*).

Transition to the video with a question. Take responses and reactions after the segment concludes.

> *How did your family manage money while you were growing up?*

 ## Video (5 minutes)

Play the "Money and Marriage" segment.

 ## Review (10 minutes)

- *Faith and finances work together.* God's gifts (intellectual, physical, financial) allow people to serve God and others, especially their families. Refer to the *Catechism* for an explanation of the "universal destination of goods" (2403–04).
- Emphasize **now** is the time to begin planning for family needs and communal responsibilities (house/car payments, education, retirement). Reserve funds and investments are not just nice to have.
- Remind the couples that the financial charts and activities in this chapter are also available online.

 ## Personal Narrative (5 minutes)

Using a specific personal experience, illustrate one or two key points to help the couples understand and respond to the content.

- Share the ups and downs of learning to budget in your marriage. Isolate an incident or two and describe the lessons you learned.
- If you experienced serious conflict over finances or financial difficulties, sharing the causes and effects with the couples in light of your faith will offer valuable insight.

34

Chapter Guides

 ## Activities (10 minutes)

Choose one or two activities as time permits; "Dealing With Debt" and "Scripture Support" are recommended. Have the couples thoughtfully consider and write down their responses before sharing with their fiancé(e). Encourage them to complete the remaining activities together and prior to their wedding so they can begin to set goals and create a shared budget.

- **"Scripture Support,"** *workbook page 92:* Offer an example from your own marriage to get them started.

- **"Guideline Budget,"** *page 97:* Couples could use this at home to create a framework for their first joint budget.

- **"Dealing With Debt,"** *pages 98–99:* Give couples time to fill in HIS and HERS then privately discuss the questions in one or two categories. Encourage them to continue on their own (see key point 2).

- **"Sample Balance Sheet/Sample Budget,"** *pages 108–111:* Couples may complete these charts on their own if desired (see key point 2). Blank copies for download and printing are available at *Liguori.org/marriage*.

 ## Reflection Questions (18 minutes)

Workbook page 106:

After each individual considers and writes his or her responses, the couple will discuss them privately. Encourage them to do more than read what they wrote. They should help one another understand their beliefs and feelings. Going in order and racing through every question is not as important as starting some real conversations that will continue and deepen over time.

Chapter Guides

Intimacy (25 minutes / 50 minutes)

Welcome and Hospitality

Greet the couples as they arrive or return. Be sure that they have the required materials, and provide supplies as needed. Begin on time.

Key Points (2 minutes)

Say, "Now let's discuss intimacy in marriage. This topic teaches us…"

1. *Intimacy reflects the Trinity* (see *workbook page 114*).
2. *Qualities and rewards of true intimacy* Connect the lists on *workbook pages 115 and 123*—there are similarities.
3. *Meeting wants, needs, and requirements* (see *workbook page 121*)

Transition to the video with a question. Take responses and reactions after the segment concludes.

> *How does your fiancé(e) let you be yourself?*

Video (5 minutes)

Play the "Intimacy" segment.

Review (8 or 13 minutes)

- Pope Francis' general audience on April 2, 2014 concisely conveys God's design for marriage—that it reflects the union of the Trinity, and of Christ and the Church. Find it on the Vatican's website, *vatican.va*.

- Ask the couples for examples of true and false intimacy, and point out the differences. (Red flags are listed on *workbook page 117*.) Then ask them how others or the culture use the word "intimacy" and compare it to marital intimacy as described here.

- Intimacy develops over time. However, the time to recognize and discuss openly any fears and red flags is *now*—before the wedding. Encourage the couples to seek counseling if anything ever threatens the relationship.

- Emphasize the difference between a want or preference and a true requirement. Christ empowers us to lay down and let go of our wants for the greater good. Because needs are essential, we should not have too many. These things may change over time and require the couple to exercise their best communication skills in regularly discussing their hopes and dreams.

Chapter Guides

🗨 Personal Narrative (5 minutes)

Using a specific personal experience, illustrate one or two key points to help the couples understand and respond to the content.

- Name a quality or two each of you found in the other early on in your relationship and how they lessened, strengthened or remained the same in your marriage.

- Describe your idea of the perfect date and the importance of finding time to be together to enjoy romantic moments. Weave this brief description into how you worked out "deal breakers" in your marriage.

- Share a couple of your wants, needs, and/or requirements and describe how you meet them with your spouse's help and/or support.

✏ Activity (5 or 10 minutes)

Have each couple choose one activity that most interests them and thoughtfully consider and write down their responses before sharing with their fiancé(e). Instruct the couples to complete the remaining activities prior to their wedding in order to complete their preparation.

"Getting to Know You," workbook page 116.

"Turning Toward Each Other," pages 119–120, key point 3: Have couples consider and write down their personal responses before sharing.

"Deal Breakers," page 122: Have the couples consider and write down their personal responses before sharing (see key point 3).

"The Perfect Date," page 125: Ask couples to create their dream date even if they have already discussed this before. Also consider having couples or leaders share their best times together. Couples can complete their writing or planning on their own.

🔍 Reflection Questions (15 minutes, depending)

Workbook page 126:

After each individual considers and writes his or her responses, the couple will discuss them privately. Encourage them to do more than read what they wrote. They should help one another understand their beliefs and feelings. Going in order and racing through every question is not as important as starting some real conversations that will continue and deepen over time.

37

Chapter Guides

Sexuality (50 minutes)

Welcome and Hospitality

Greet the couples as they arrive or return. Be sure that they have the required materials, and provide supplies as needed. Begin on time.

★ Key Points (2 minutes)

Say, "Now we will talk about sexuality in marriage. This topic teaches us…"

1. *God's design for sex and sexuality* (*Theology of the Body* is summarized on *workbook page 131*.)
2. *The dual purpose of intercourse* ("procreation and mutual love," see *workbook page 133*)
3. *The morality of sexual acts and practices*

Transition to the video with a question. Take responses and reactions after the segment concludes.

If your sexuality were a flame, how would you describe it: A matchstick? A bonfire?

▶ Video (4 minutes)

Play the "Sexuality" segment.

♥ Review (9 minutes)

- Address the nature of marital love with respect to our bodies and the union of spouses as reflecting our union with God. In his *Theology of the Body,* Pope John Paul II speaks of the "nuptial meaning" of our bodies. In freely giving of themselves to one another, wives and husbands share the Creator's love with each other, which brings fruitfulness to their union.

- Sexuality in marriage is more than the act of intercourse. Loving gestures, gentle touches, and kind words enhance marital intimacy and sexuality. Focus on the moral perspective, with regard to intentions and choices.

- Refer to the sexual practices on *workbook page 135* and point out those that may damage a marriage (addiction, abuse, pornography, etc.). Emphasize the importance of getting professional help now if any serious concerns are present.

Personal Narrative (5 minutes)

Using a specific personal experience, illustrate one or two key points to help the couples understand and respond to the content.

- Keep your story focused on the general sense of the holiness of your sexual relationship with your spouse. If you have studied *Theology of the Body,* you may want to elaborate on what effect it has had on your marital relationship.
- Choose an activity you will be introducing in the session and give examples from your marriage.

Activity (10 minutes)

Introduce "Getting to Know You" and have the couples write their responses before sharing with their fiancé(e). *Ask them to thoughtfully consider each activity and to avoid simply jotting down silly or suggestive responses.* Stress the importance of completing the remaining activities together and prior to the wedding so that their marital relations will begin on the best foundation—a holy one.

"Getting to Know You," *workbook page 132.*

"Sexual Feelings," *page 134*: This activity requires private and very honest discussions. Encourage the couples to be open and vulnerable to each other in these areas.

"Sexual Wholeness," *page 137*: Encourage the couples to be open and honest as they share their responses. Remind them that preferences and needs will develop and change over time, so flexibility and continued communication are necessary.

Reflection Questions (20 minutes)

Workbook page 138:

After each individual considers and writes his or her responses, the couple will discuss them privately. Encourage them to do more than read what they wrote. They should help one another understand their beliefs and feelings. Going in order and racing through every question is not as important as starting some real conversations that will continue and deepen over time.

Chapter Guides

Natural Family Planning (25 minutes / 50 minutes)

Welcome and Hospitality

Greet the couples as they arrive or return. Be sure they have the required materials, and provide supplies as needed. *A Bible will be needed for some of the activities in this chapter.* Begin on time.

⭐ Key Points (2 minutes)

Say, "Now we will introduce natural family planning. This chapter teaches us about…"

1. *Approaching fertility and parenthood as a Christian couple* (The activity on *workbook page 143* features biblical parents.)
2. *Anatomy and the menstrual cycle* (see *workbook pages 144–148*)
3. *Methods and advantages of NFP* (The chart on *workbook pages 152–153* is also available at *Liguori.org/marriage*.)

Transition to the video with a question. Take responses and reactions after the segment concludes.

> **What exposure have you had to natural family planning?**

▶ Video (5 minutes)

Play the "Natural Family Planning" segment.

– Tip –

Prior to this session, ask your parish or diocese for information on the NFP resources in your area. Sometimes a speaker will come and address the couples. If so, adjust the session schedule to include time for the instructor's presentation or personal witnesses from couples who are or who have practiced NFP.

♥ Review (3 or 8 minutes)

- Remind couples that God is present in their lives and has a plan for their marriage and family that may or may not match their hopes and expectations. Walking together in faith, they can grow to accept God's will and take steps to cooperate with it.

- A mutual understanding of each other's relative fertility will improve the spouses' sexual satisfaction and general confidence in family planning.

- Through handouts or a guest speaker, provide the couples with NFP options that are available locally.

Chapter Guides

Personal Narrative (5 minutes)

Using a specific personal experience, illustrate one or two key points to help the couples understand and respond to the content.

- A brief story about your own knowledge of NFP prior to marriage versus what you learned along the way may encourage the couples to make an appointment with NFP providers prior to the wedding.
- If you have experienced infertility, adoption, or miscarriage, consider sharing the feelings, outcomes, and effects on your marriage or children.

Activities (10 or 15 minutes)

Introduce "Scripture Support" and read the first passage aloud. Invite the couples to share responses and reactions with the group. Continue with the remaining three readings. If time permits, introduce "Getting to Know You" and/or "NFP Training." Instruct them to complete all of the activities prior to their wedding in order to complete their preparation.

"**Scripture Support**," *workbook page 143*, key point 1.

"**Getting to Know You**," *page 149*.

"**The NFP Lifestyle**," *page 154*.

"**NFP Training**," *page 155*: Review the three steps as you distribute information on local NFP instructors.

Reflection Questions (15 minutes, depending)

Workbook page 156:

After each individual considers and writes his or her responses, the couple will discuss them privately. Encourage them to do more than read what they wrote. They should help one another understand their beliefs and feelings. Going in order and racing through every question is not as important as starting some real conversations that will continue and deepen over time.

Chapter Guides

Children and Parenting (50 minutes)

Welcome and Hospitality

Greet the couples as they arrive or return. Be sure that they have the required materials, and provide supplies as needed. Begin on time.

Key Points (2 minutes)

Say, "Now let's discuss children and parenting. This chapter teaches us that…"

1. *Children are a gift to their parents and society* (see *workbook page 161*).
2. *Parenting styles may vary based on gender and personality.* Strive for a combination that is effective and meaningful for the entire family.
3. *Families bond by working, playing, and praying together.* (Tips and ideas are on *workbook pages 170–172*.)

Transition to the video with a question. Take responses and reactions after the segment concludes.

How do you react to seeing young children in church or in prayer?

Video (6 minutes)

Play the "Children and Parenting" segment.

Review (10 minutes)

- Children are unique persons with God-given dignity and individual needs. Parenting involves balancing the needs of the family members within human, social, logistic, and time constraints.

- While our faith mandates certain behaviors and restricts others, it doesn't teach the "one right way" to parent or discipline. Parents are free to adapt their lifestyle and house rules for the good and advancement of the entire family within their culture and circumstances.

- Vatican II recognized the importance of raising and educating children: "The family is, so to speak, the domestic church. In it parents should, by their word and example, be the first preachers of the faith to their children; they should encourage them in the vocation which is proper to each of them…" (*Lumen Gentium*, 11).

- Pope Francis has also spoken passionately about the family. Family life is where we first learn to love, forgive, and build relationships. His statements are on the Vatican's website, *vatican.va*.

Chapter Guides

💬 Personal Narrative (5 minutes)

Using a specific personal experience, illustrate key points to help the couples understand and respond to the content.

- Describe the similarities and differences in your parenting styles in one important example with your children.
- What difficult situation have you experienced as a parent?
- What Scripture passages have supported you as parents and have given you hope for your children's lives?

✏️ Activity (10 minutes)

Introduce "What Would You Do?" and discuss some solutions as a group. Instruct the couples to complete *all* the activities prior to the wedding in order to complete their preparation.

"**Baby Pictures,**" *workbook page 162.*

"**Scripture Support,**" *page 165.*

"**What Would You Do?**" *pages 168–169,* key point 2: Responses will vary, and couples should be able to explain their reasoning. Suggested answers are below; you may also have personal experiences or solutions to share.

1. *If I were Brayden's parent, I would…* Offer him a ready or healthy choice, distract him with another activity, or he may be able to set his place or help prepare a dish.

2. *If I were Paul's parent, I would…* If he was reminded and managed his time poorly, he may be culpable, and missing the party would be a natural consequence of his choices. If the circumstances were exceptional, you may offer to help.

3. *If I were Veronica's parent, I would…* While she is legally an adult, she is not living independently. Parents have the right to establish standards and limits within the home and to inquire about their child's life and offer advice regarding the avoidance of sin.

4. *If I were their parent, I would…* For Catholics, weekly (Sunday) Mass is obligatory, a precept of the Church (*CCC* 2042). Perhaps one parent could attend the recital while the other attends the vigil Mass, leaving Sunday morning to the other parent and the girls.

Family Life Chart *page 173:* If time permits, couples or leaders may share a few of their answers with the group (see key point 3).

🔍 Reflection Questions (17 minutes)

Workbook page 174:

After writing their responses, the couples will discuss them privately, helping each other understand their beliefs and feelings and beginning some real conversations that will continue and deepen over time.

Chapter Guides

Cohabitation (25 minutes / 50 minutes)

Welcome and Hospitality

Greet the couples as they arrive or return. Be sure that they have the required materials, and provide supplies as needed. Begin on time.

Key Points (2 minutes)

Say, "Now let's talk about cohabitation. This chapter will help you grow in three ways:"

1. *The truth about marriage, sex, and Catholic teaching* (see *workbook pages 180–181*)
2. *Debunking the myths of cohabitation and compatibility* (Three myths are discussed on *pages 183–187*.)
3. *Transitioning to marriage and chastity* (see *workbook pages 188–190*)

Transition to the video with a question. Take responses and reactions after the segment concludes.

What is the difference between living together and being married? What do the vows mean to you, to your fiancé(e) and to God?

Video (6 minutes)

Play the "Cohabitation" segment.

Review (7 minutes)

- To address concerns or criticisms of Church teaching, keep in mind the sacramental nature of marriage. Review the authentic meanings of marital love and fidelity and explain the impossibility of "trying out" a lifelong commitment.

- Illustrate what makes sacramental marriage attractive and the value of committing yourself fully to another person. Marriage preparation allows couples the time and guidance to explore the nature and depth of their love.

Personal Narrative (5 minutes, depending)

Consider sharing why you personally chose (not) to cohabit before marriage, or present examples from your experience of the challenges and potential damage of cohabitation on relationships.

– Tip –

Making yourself or another parish resource available outside of the sessions for guidance or counseling is especially beneficial to couples in sensitive or unique circumstances.

44

Chapter Guides

✏️ Activities (10 or 15 minutes)

Introduce "True Love" and give ample time for personal reflection prior to calling the couples to each other or the group. If time permits, introduce "We Go Together." Stress the importance of completing *all* the activities prior to the wedding so that their marriage begins on a strong foundation.

"True Love," *workbook page 182:*
Suggested answers are below.
Paying for meals or bills / Giving gifts...
Is real when it expresses generosity.
Is fake when it becomes a quid pro quo or justification for dominance.
Sharing pet- or child-care duties...
Is real when it supports a loved one's need for independence.
Is fake when it replaces the rightful duties of the pet owner or parent or interferes with the child's relationship with either parent.
Staying late or overnight...
Is real when it expresses mutual desire or emotional support, say, during a difficult time.
Is fake when it leads to possessiveness or codependency or interferes with one's responsibilities.
Spending time with an adult of the opposite sex...
Is real when it fosters healthy friendships.
Is fake when it becomes an occasion of sin, specifically lust.

Engaging in sexual activity with less than full interest or desire...
Is real when it shows trust and submission between spouses (and may lead to arousal).
Is fake when it is a sign of coercion or abuse.

"We Go Together," *page 186:*
Each person needs to assess their responses and scores privately. Encourage them to be honest in rating the statements and sharing their scores when they have time to consider the implications thoroughly.

"Your Story of Salvation," *page 190:*
This activity is best done on their own when each individual can thoughtfully prepare their response.

🔍 Reflection Questions (15 minutes, depending)

Workbook page 192:

After writing their responses, the couples will discuss them privately, helping each other understand their beliefs and feelings and beginning some real conversations that will continue and deepen over time.

– Tip –
The USCCB site *ForYourMarriage.org* offers updated reports from studies on the effects of cohabitation.

45

Chapter Guides

Annulment and Convalidation (20 minutes / 25 minutes)

Welcome and Hospitality

Greet the couples as they arrive or return. Be sure they have the required materials, and provide supplies as needed. Begin on time.

⭐ Key Points (2 minutes)

Say, "Now we will discuss the processes of annulment and convalidation. This chapter teaches us that…"

1. *Christian marriage is called to be permanent.* A brief history is found on *workbook pages 198–199.*
2. *The essence of the annulment process is identical across the globe.* The basic steps are listed on *pages 200–201.*
3. *Civil marriages are recognized by the Church through convalidation.* Learn how it works on *page 204.*

Transition to the video with a question. Take responses and reactions after the segment concludes.

Besides the Church, who else has a stake in your marriage?

▶ Video (5 minutes)

Play the "Annulment and Convalidation" segment.

♥ Review (3 minutes)

- All couples requesting marriage in the Church must present themselves to the pastor, who will determine their marriage-preparation requirements, including annulment.

- This chapter reinforces the importance of a sacramentally valid ceremony and Church teachings on marriage that are addressed in the Theology and Rite chapters.

> **– Tip –**
> This topic and the chapter activities may be difficult for those with little to no training in annulments. If couples have concerns or questions that go beyond your resources, seek guidance from the priest or deacon.

> **– Tip –**
> A title card just after the 4-minute mark signals the beginning of the video presentation specific to convalidation.

Chapter Guides

💬 Personal Narrative (optional)

Only offer stories from your own experience with divorce and annulment.

✏️ Activity (5 minutes)

Introduce "Unveiling the Truth" and have the couples respond to the questions before sharing the correct answers. Instruct the couples to complete "If I Knew Then…" prior to their wedding.

"Unveiling the Truth," *workbook page 197:*

1. **False.** Catholics who remarry without receiving an annulment are guilty of adultery and should not receive the Eucharist. However, they should remain active in their parish and seek support, reconciliation, and an annulment of their prior marriage whenever possible.

2. **False (with a caveat).** The Church recognizes all civil and common-law marriages between one man and one woman as valid, though not necessarily sacramental, unless proven otherwise. The key exception to this is when one of the spouses is baptized Catholic. In those cases, that party must receive a dispensation or seek convalidation for the marriage to be valid.

3. **False.** Because natural marriages are valid (see above), even non-Catholic spouses need to receive an annulment before "remarrying" in the Catholic Church. This is perplexing to some but truly speaks to the truth and value of marriage.

4. **False (Well, it depends).** This is discussed briefly at the opening of the annulment process section on *workbook page 199*.

"If I Knew Then…" *page 205:*
As difficult as it may be, earnestly ask them to engage and complete this activity. Stress the importance of sharing their responses with each other fully and privately; the discussions that ensue are necessary.

🔍 Reflection Questions (5 or 10 minutes)

Workbook page 206:

After writing their responses, the couples will discuss them privately, helping each other understand their beliefs and feelings and beginning some real conversations that will continue and deepen over time.

Chapter Guides

Interchurch and Interfaith Marriages (25 minutes / 40 minutes)

Welcome and Hospitality

Greet the couples as they arrive or return. Be sure they have the required materials, and provide supplies as needed. Begin on time.

★ Key Points (2 minutes)

Say, "Now we will discuss marriages in which one spouse is not Catholic. This chapter teaches us…"

1. *The Catholic Church values mixed-religion marriages*. In fact, Catholics marry non-Catholics 40% of the time.
2. *Common challenges surround the wedding and children*. The workbook addresses them on *pages 213–219*.
3. *Let your communities guide and support you*.

Transition to the video with a question. Take responses and reactions after the segment concludes.

Have you attended a religious service or event with your fiancé(e)? What interchurch and interfaith couples do you know?

▶ Video (5 minutes)

Play the "Interchurch and Interfaith Marriages" segment.

♥ Review (3 or 8 minutes)

- Help the mixed-religion couples identify the type of marriage they are preparing for. Make sure they know whether their union will be sacramental and that they will need a dispensation for the marriage to be valid.

- Allow the couples to introduce themselves and their backgrounds to the group. The non-Catholics may be able to enlighten you and others on their faith community and views on marriage.

- Hand out basic contact information for the parish as well as any local resource that puts the couples in touch with their Catholic community and begins to build their spiritual network.

💬 Personal Narrative (5 minutes, optional)

Offer from your own experience how your relationship has become stronger by trying to resolve conflicts over differences in faith. The topic may be expanded to include religious differences in your families of origin.

Chapter Guides

✏️ Activity (10 minutes)

Introduce "Defining Your Faith" and have each individual write down their responses before sharing. Then offer couples the Catholic definitions below*. Instruct the couples to complete the remaining activities prior to their wedding in order to complete their preparation.

"Defining Your Faith," *workbook page 211:* Compare and discuss the terms in the sidebar as a group. Never hold an individual up as an expert or leave religious or technical definitions up for interpretation.

- **Covenant:** Sacred agreement that cannot be broken (e.g. between God and humanity and between spouses)
- **Faith:** Belief, trust in, and "acceptance of the word of another," such as divine faith in God
- **Grace:** A supernatural gift that allows one to see God and prepare for heaven. *Actual grace* is "divine assistance." *Sanctifying grace* is "being infused by God…a participation in the divine life."
- **Justice:** The virtue by which people "give everyone his or her rightful due." It directs right actions and right relationships.
- **Law:** "An ordinance of reason for the common good." Catholics distinguish among natural law, civil law, divine law ("This eternal law embraces both the physical and moral laws."), and Canon Law.
- **Sacrament:** A tangible sign, "instituted by Jesus Christ, by which invisible grace and inward sanctification" are effected. Catholics teach the seven sacraments: **baptism, confirmation, Eucharist, penance, anointing, holy orders,** and **marriage.**

*Quotes from **Modern Catholic Dictionary**, Fr. John Hardon, SJ. © 2000, Eternal Life.

"Scripture Support," *page 215.*

"Perspectives on Marriage and Family," *page 220.*

🔍 Reflection Questions (10–15 minutes, depending)

Workbook page 221:

After each individual considers and writes his or her responses, the couple will discuss them privately. Encourage them to help one another understand their beliefs and feelings and to start some real conversations that will continue and deepen over time.

Chapter Guides

Military Marriage (25 minutes / 40 minutes)

Welcome and Hospitality

Greet the couples as they arrive or return. Be sure they have the required materials, and provide supplies as needed. Begin on time.

★ Key Points (2 minutes)

Say, "Now we will discuss marriage when it includes active military service. This chapter teaches us about…"

1. *Living the military life as a couple*
2. *Dealing with separation, relocation, and injury (Workbook pages 229–234 offer tips and suggestions.)*
3. *Using the resources and support available to you*

Transition to the video with a question. Take responses and reactions after the segment concludes.

When you think of the military, who or what comes to mind?

▶ Video (5 minutes)

Play the "Military Marriage" segment.

♥ Review (8 minutes)

- Couples who are dating through active military service already have experiences and expectations surrounding their relationship and the related position or duty. Remind them that both of their perspectives are important and needed to build unity, understanding, and trust. Desires, fears, and needs must be communicated, even if their partner doesn't share or agree with them or if he or she can't address them right away or alone.

- Remind them that God is the one who began this great adventure between the two of them—and he is the one who will unite and bind them together forever.

- Recall biblical characters who risked their lives and/or traveled far in the name of discipleship: Abraham, Joseph, Moses, Daniel, John the Baptist, Stephen. There are also countless saints, martyrs, and military patrons from which to draw. This may lead naturally into the "Scripture Support" activity.

Chapter Guides

💬 Personal Narrative (optional)

Leaders with military experience will have specific events to draw from. Those without may need to rely on a discussion with the couples who are willing to share their own challenges and resolutions, as well as direct them to their military chaplain or contact.

✏️ Activities (10 minutes)

Have each couple choose one activity that most interests them and thoughtfully consider and write down their responses before sharing with their fiancé(e). Instruct the couples to complete the remaining activities prior to their wedding in order to complete their preparation.

- **"Chain of Command,"** *workbook page 228:* If the couples will share their responses with the group, acknowledge the consistent struggle to weigh multiple authorities that may or may not compete. Ask everyone to remain sensitive to different religious and political leanings.
- **"My Military Life,"** *page 233,* see key point 1.
- **"Scripture Support,"** *page 237.*

🔍 Reflection Questions (15 minutes, depending)

Workbook page 238:

After each individual considers and writes his or her responses, the couple will discuss them privately. Encourage them to help one another understand their beliefs and feelings and to start some real conversations that will continue and deepen over time.

— Tip —

While those serving in the military have unique challenges in marriage and family life, similar critical challenges are also present in families when one spouse travels frequently, job transfers occur across state or country lines, or home life is disrupted by a crisis. In such circumstances, these families have an opportunity to bring their faith into a new environment. When others see the value a couple places on their marriage and family, God's unconditional love becomes visible and alive in the world.

Closing Prayer Service

(25 minutes / 30 minutes)

*This prayer service presumes the leaders are a married couple.
If not, a single leader may simply lead the reflections prayerfully.*

Welcome and Hospitality

Greet the couples as they arrive or return. Be sure *you* have the required materials (see page 9 and tip, at right). If the group is moving to the chapel or another location, make sure each person is sitting next to his or her fiancé(e). Begin on time.

Transition to the video with a question. Explain to the couples that their answers will come later and in their daily words and actions, both now and after their wedding.

*How would you describe the love between your fiancé(e) and you?
How can you best express that love?*

▶ Video (3 minutes)

Play the "Conclusion and Credits" segment.

> **– Tip –**
>
> Most couples must present proof that they completed their marriage preparation. Your parish or diocese also may provide its own documentation. Have these and all necessary forms or next steps ready for couples before they leave the final session.
>
> *Your Marriage* offers a certificate at *Liguori.org/marriage* that serves to formalize the program experience. Each couple may be presented with their certificate at the end of the final session. Even with a large group, this can be a simple ceremony. Incorporating it into a Mass would also be appropriate. In this context, certificates would be presented after Communion.

Scripture Reading (2 minutes)

Leader 1: The love of God surrounds us as a warm, gentle light. We see God's light in one another. Our God, who loves without judgment, asks us to love one another with patience and gentleness, always ready to forgive and seek forgiveness. May the light of Christ radiate through our lives and our marriages.

Leader 2: A reading from the first Letter of St. Paul to the Corinthians (13:4–8):

Brothers and sisters:
Love is patient, love is kind.
It is not jealous, it is not pompous,
it is not inflated, it is not rude,
it does not seek its own interests,
it is not quick-tempered, it does not brood over injury,
it does not rejoice over wrongdoing
but rejoices with the truth.
It bears all things, believes all things,
hopes all things, endures all things.
Love never fails.

Reflection on the Vows (3 minutes)

Leader 1: On the day you say, "I do," you may be understandably distracted or overwhelmed. Listen now to what you will be asked to promise, that you may be better able to take the words to heart.

Leader 2: At your wedding, the presider will ask you three questions:

1. *Have you come together freely and without reservation to give yourselves to each other in marriage?*

2. *Will you love and honor each other as man and wife for the rest of your lives?*

3. *Will you accept children lovingly from God and bring them up according to the law of Christ and his Church?*

Closing Prayer Service

Leader 1: After you respond affirmatively to each question, you will turn to one another, join hands, and declare your consent: (Leaders face each other, hold hands, and take turns reading slowly, inserting their names in the blanks.)

I, _____, take you, _____ to be my [wife/husband],
I promise to be true to you in good times and in bad,
in sickness and in health.
I will love you and honor you all the days of my life.

Leader 2: You will then hear these words:

You have declared your consent before the Church.
May the Lord in his goodness strengthen your consent
and bless you both with the Spirit of Wisdom.
What God has joined, men must not divide.

All: **Amen.**

Leader 1: Let us pray together using the words that Jesus taught us:

Our Father, who art in heaven,
hallowed be thy name;
thy kingdom come;
thy will be done on earth as it is in heaven.
Give us this day our daily bread;
and forgive us our trespasses
as we forgive those who trespass against us;
and lead us not into temptation,
but deliver us from evil.
Amen.

Sign of Peace (2 minutes)

Leader 2: Turn now to your beloved and take his or her hand. As you offer each other a sign of peace, share what you have learned or gained in your preparation for marriage as well as your hopes and dreams for your life ahead.

(The couples will embrace and/or offer another gesture of affection. Wait for the commotion to subside, then continue.)

Presentation of Certificates (5 or 10 minutes)

Explain that the certificate emphasizes the Church's desire for the welfare of families and reminds the couple that they never journey alone. Along with their certificate and/or letter, each couple will receive paper on which each person can write a love letter to his or her fiancé(e). The letters should be written privately and delivered on the wedding day or another special occasion. The letter is both a gift to their marriage and a sign and early fruit of their love and fidelity.

Call the names of each couple who completed the program aloud as they come forward. Present each couple with their certificate and/or letter, evaluation form, and love letter supplies. When all have returned to their seats, dismiss the group, instructing them to complete their evaluation form prior to departing.

Dismissal (10 minutes)

Leader 2: Go now in peace to love and serve God and each other.

All: **Alleluia, Alleluia.**

Maintaining an Effective Program

Building Community

Marriage preparation benefits from proper evaluation by both the participants and the facilitators. Furthermore, both the program content and the leaders' presentations need to be evaluated. Parishes and dioceses may have forms that suit their particular needs. *Your Marriage* provides an evaluation form for couples and another for leaders in this guide and online at *Liguori.org/marriage*.

Once the responses have been gathered, the effectiveness of the program and material can be reviewed, and clarification, supplemental information, or additional training can be provided to strengthen your parish or diocese's overall ministry.

In addition to regular evaluation, parishes and dioceses can maintain the effectiveness of their marriage-preparation program through:

1. Follow-up with the couples who participated in the program.
2. Collaboration with leaders across dioceses to share ideas and recruit facilitators.

The U.S. Conference of Catholic Bishops (USCCB) have emphasized the need to spread the good news about marriage in our culture. **Keep in touch with the couples, perhaps before their wedding day** or near their first anniversary. Since many couples do not live in the parish in which they were married, all parishes can extend the hospitality of marriage preparation to the couples celebrating their first anniversary by inviting them to a special Mass held once a year. This is an easy opportunity to gather more feedback and distribute or perform a first-anniversary exercise as a group.

— *Tip* —

Your Marriage and Liguori Publications offer and list additional resources online. Leaders are encouraged to use them as appropriate. Parishes and dioceses should also address any unique demographic or cultural trends that affect their region.

Prayer for Marriage-preparation Leaders

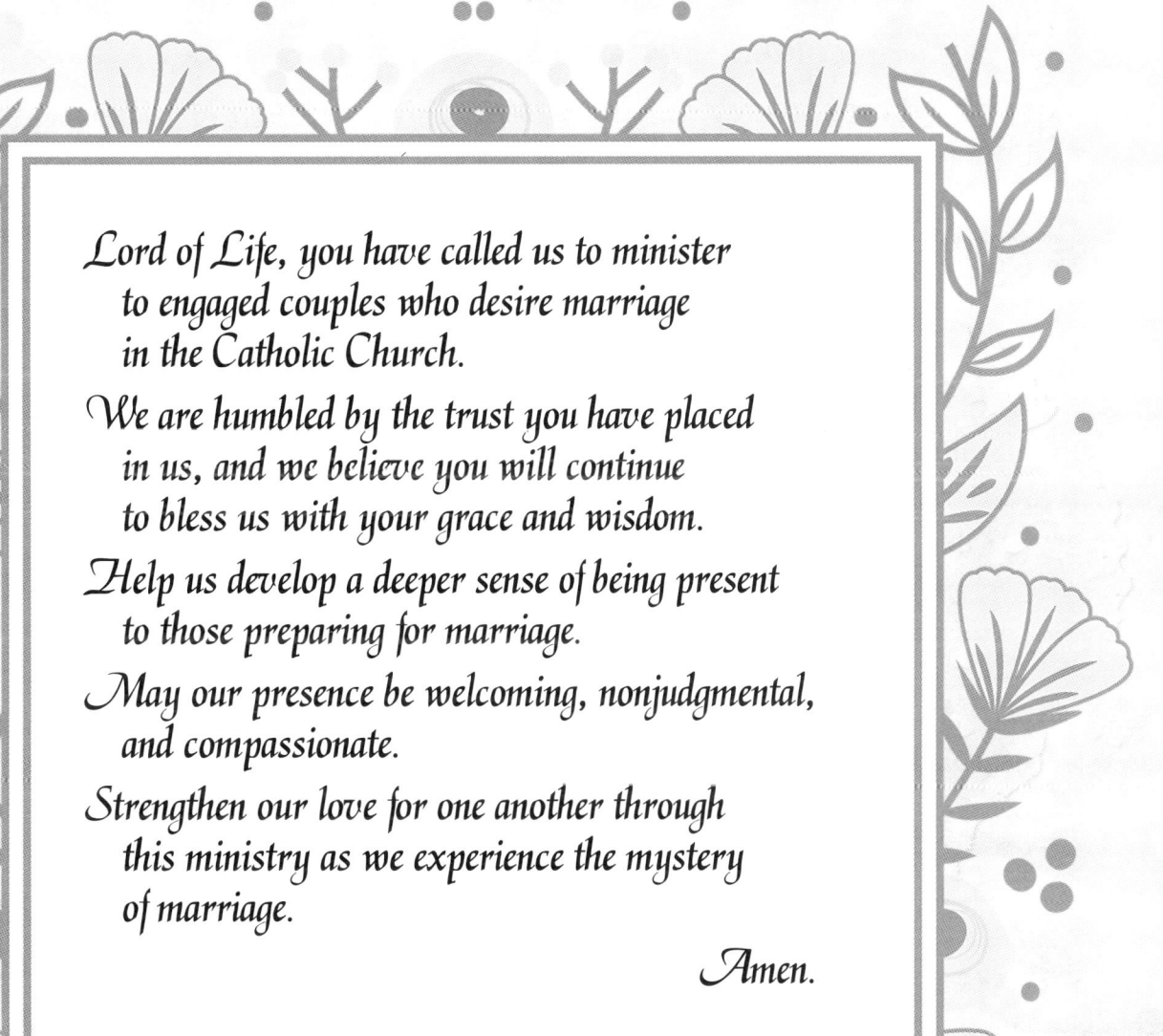

Lord of Life, you have called us to minister
to engaged couples who desire marriage
in the Catholic Church.

We are humbled by the trust you have placed
in us, and we believe you will continue
to bless us with your grace and wisdom.

Help us develop a deeper sense of being present
to those preparing for marriage.

May our presence be welcoming, nonjudgmental,
and compassionate.

Strengthen our love for one another through
this ministry as we experience the mystery
of marriage.

Amen.

PARTICIPANT'S Evaluation Form — *To be completed by both partners separately*

Participant's Evaluation Form

Tell us about yourself and how you prepared for marriage.

I am: Male ___   Female ___   Age _____

I used *Your Marriage* (check all that apply):

- ☐ With my priest, deacon, or wedding presider
- ☐ Privately with (a) sponsor couple(s)
- ☐ In a group/class setting
- ☐ During a retreat
- ☐ Through my parish
- ☐ Through my fiancé(e)'s parish
- ☐ Through my diocese
- ☐ Through my fiancé(e)'s diocese
- ☐ Through a military chaplaincy
- ☐ Other (please describe)

Did you know your facilitator prior to your engagement?   ___ Yes   ___ No

Were you given separate/additional resources to read and discuss?   ___ Yes   ___ No

Which of these chapters did you use?
(Check all that apply.)

- ☐ Cohabitation
- ☐ Annulment and Convalidation
- ☐ Interchurch and Interfaith Marriages
- ☐ Military Marriage
- ☐ I didn't use any of these chapters.

Please rate the following using the scale below:
1 = poor   2 = bad   3 = good   4 = great

a. The marriage-preparation program overall
   1   2   3   4

b. The structure of the program
   1   2   3   4

c. The sponsor couple(s) and/or leader(s)
   1   2   3   4

d. The sessions and/or retreat
   1   2   3   4
   (This includes extras like icebreakers, activities, testimonies, and refreshments.)

e. Session/Retreat location(s), dates, and times
   1   2   3   4

f. The workbook chapters
   1   2   3   4

g. The chapter activities
   1   2   3   4

h. The video (if applicable)
   1   2   3   4

i. Separate/additional resources (if applicable)
   1   2   3   4

Tell us more about the *Your Marriage* program.
What topic or chapter helped you the **most**?

What topic or chapter helped you the **least**?

Does anything seem missing from the program?
___ Yes   ___ No   If so, please describe.

Liguori PUBLICATIONS

To be completed by both partners separately   **PARTICIPANT'S Evaluation Form**

Please respond to the statements below using the following scale:
1 = none or very little   2 = some
3 = more   4 = much greater

After using *Your Marriage*...

a. my understanding of marriage and the wedding vows is: 1   2   3   4

b. my understanding of the Rite of Marriage and wedding ceremony is: 1   2   3   4

c. my willingness and readiness to commit to a lifelong marriage is: 1   2   3   4

d. my willingness to continue growing in faith with my spouse is: 1   2   3   4

e. my willingness to recommend *Your Marriage* to other couples is: 1   2   3   4

Please respond to the statements below using the following scale:
1 = much less   2 = less
3 = more   4 = much more

I wish there were ____ prayer in *Your Marriage*.

I wish there were ____ Scripture in *Your Marriage*.

I wish there were ____ *Theology of the Body* in *Your Marriage*.

I wish there were ____ online/downloadable material for *Your Marriage*.

I wish my costs for participating in *Your Marriage* were ____.

Please rate the *Your Marriage: Program DVD* on the following scales:

Engaging   4   3   2   1   Boring
Enlightening   4   3   2   1   Offensive
Fresh/Unique   4   3   2   1   Bland or Dated

Tell us your thoughts as you complete your marriage preparation.

That *Your Marriage* received an *Imprimatur* was important to me.   ___ True   ___ False

That *Your Marriage* was approved by my parish/diocese was important to me.
   ___ True   ___ False

That *Your Marriage* had a video component was important to me.   ___ True   ___ False

I was given adequate time to complete the questions and activities in the workbook.
   ___ True   ___ False

I will complete my preparation for marriage by reading and discussing any part of the material not fully covered in class with my fiancé(e).
   ___ True   ___ False

I feel prepared to confer and receive the sacrament of marriage.   ___ True   ___ False

Would you like to share anything else with your sponsor couple(s), presider, or parish?

Please return a copy of this evaluation to your facilitator or presider. You should receive a certificate or letter of completion prior to your wedding.

Liguori Publications welcomes your feedback and comments, including copies of this evaluation. You may email us at Liguori@liguori.org. God bless you and your ministry!

LEADER'S Evaluation Form *To be completed by each facilitator separately*

Leader's Evaluation Form

Tell us about yourself and your marriage-preparation program.

1. I am: Male ____   Female ____   Age ____

2. I used *Your Marriage* (check all that apply):
   - ☐ As a priest, deacon, or wedding presider
   - ☐ As a member of a sponsor couple
   - ☐ As a group leader, retreat director, or marriage-prep coordinator
   - ☐ With individual couples
   - ☐ In a small-group setting
   - ☐ In a large-group setting
   - ☐ Through my parish
   - ☐ Through my diocese
   - ☐ Through a military chaplaincy
   - ☐ Other (please describe) _____

3. How many of your couples did you know prior to the program?
   ____ None   ____ Some   ____ Most   ____ All

4. Did you provide separate/additional resources for study and discussion?
   ____ Yes   ____ No   If so, what were they?

5. Which of these chapters did you assign and use? (Check all that apply.)
   - ☐ Cohabitation
   - ☐ Annulment and Convalidation
   - ☐ Interchurch and Interfaith Marriages
   - ☐ Military Marriage
   - ☐ I didn't use any of these chapters.

6. What topic or chapter was most effective and meaningful? Please explain.

7. What topic or chapter was least effective and meaningful? Please explain.

8. Does anything seem missing from the program? ____ Yes   ____ No
   If so, please describe.

LEADER'S Evaluation Form — *To be completed by each facilitator separately*

9. **Please rate the following using the scale below:**
   1 = poor   2 = bad   3 = good   4 = great

   a. The marriage-preparation program overall — 1 2 3 4
   b. The costs of the program — 1 2 3 4
   c. The structure of the program — 1 2 3 4
   d. The training given by the director, parish, or diocese — 1 2 3 4
   e. The time given to review the material, prepare personal narratives, and plan for sessions — 1 2 3 4
   f. The session/retreat schedules and time allotted — 1 2 3 4
   g. The session/retreat location(s), dates, and times — 1 2 3 4
   h. The couple(s)' attendance and preparedness — 1 2 3 4
   i. The couple(s)' willingness to learn and participate (This includes icebreakers, activities and questions) — 1 2 3 4
   j. The program's use of prayer — 1 2 3 4
   k. The program's use of Scripture and doctrine — 1 2 3 4
   l. The workbook activities — 1 2 3 4
   m. The quality of the video content — 1 2 3 4
   n. The video's engagement value and accessibility — 1 2 3 4

10. **Please respond to the statements below using the following scale:**
    1 = none or very little   2 = some   3 = more   4 = much greater

    After facilitating *Your Marriage*...

    a. my understanding of marriage is: — 1 2 3 4
    b. my understanding of the Catholic faith is: — 1 2 3 4
    c. my commitment to my marriage or vocation is: — 1 2 3 4
    d. my awareness of my spouse's and/or my faith is: — 1 2 3 4
    e. my willingness to continue growing in faith with my spouse is: — 1 2 3 4
    f. my willingness to recommend *Your Marriage* to other parishes and dioceses is: — 1 2 3 4

11. Would you like to share anything else with your director, parish, diocesan office, or Liguori Publications?

Liguori Publications welcomes your feedback and comments, including copies of this evaluation. You may email us at Liguori@liguori.org. God bless you and your ministry!

Liguori PUBLICATIONS

FIRST AID FOR FAMILIES

PRACTICAL HELP FOR LIFE'S MESSY HOLINESS!

Family, the Church and the Real World

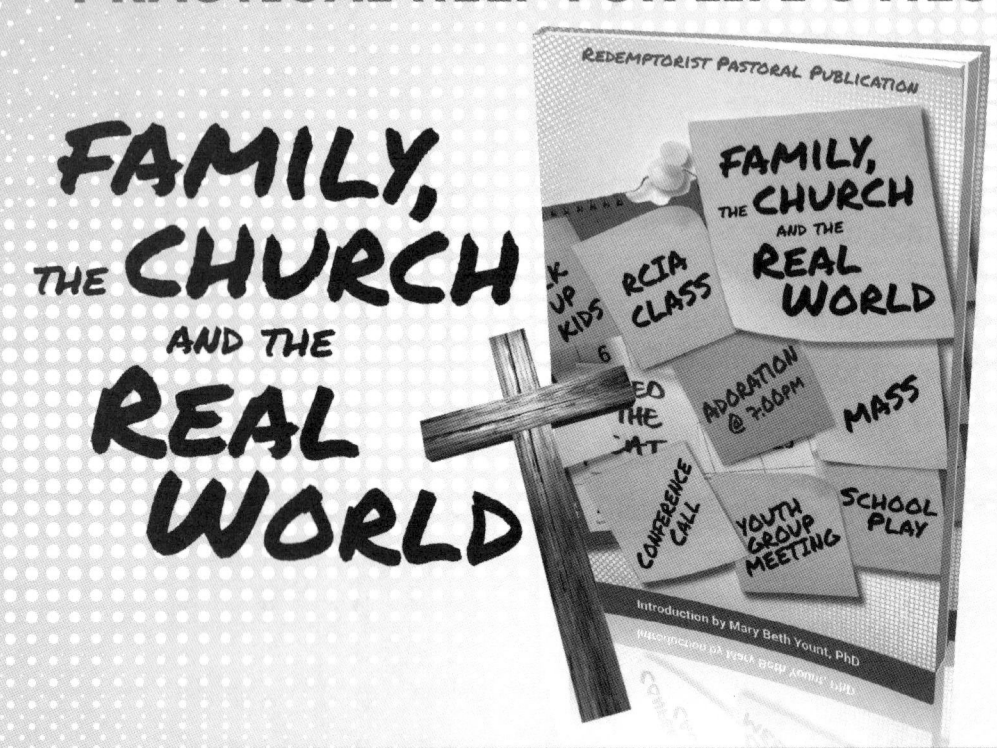

The Popcaks, Christopher West, and other Catholic family-life experts join forces to help families put Christ first.

144 pages • 826207
$14.99

CATHOLIC UPDATE

This full-color, four-page newsletter uses everyday language to help people connect Church teaching and current topics to everyday life. Provide quality Catholic content to your parishioners through digital and print subscriptions.

TOPICS:
- Sacraments
- Ethics and morality
- Scripture
- Spirituality and prayer
- Saints
- Social justice/Catholic social teaching
- Liturgical year and seasons
- Family life
- Catholic practices and devotions

Visit us at liguori.org/catholic-update
to see a full listing of all *Catholic Update* titles.

Liguori.org • 800-325-9521

Liguori PUBLICATIONS

LIGUORIAN MAGAZINE

From Beloved to Bold
Liguorian magazine is even more relevant today

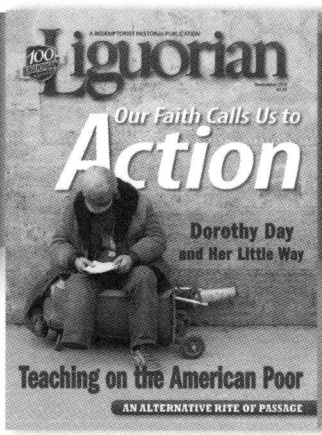

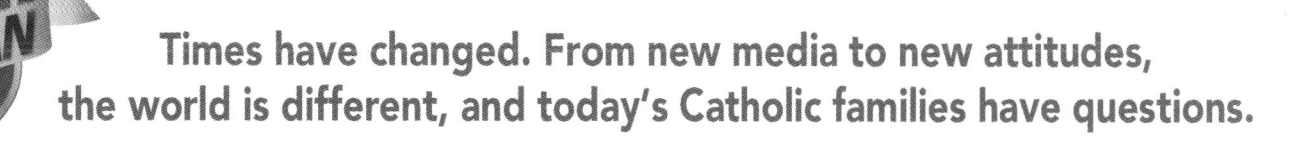

100 LIGUORIAN years

Times have changed. From new media to new attitudes, the world is different, and today's Catholic families have questions.

Liguorian provides answers. This beloved Redemptorist pastoral magazine helps your staff, your teachers, and your parishioners live their faith in the world.

Liguorian has also changed since its start in 1913—it's still beloved, but also bolder, with new resources for your busy life:

- Print subscription now comes with access to the Online Digital Edition
- Liguorian App for iOS allows access to a full subscription or to single issues and offers sharing and other features

Don't wait! Save money today on discounted bulk subscriptions.
Just call 866-848-2492.
For a free digital issue, visit Liguorian.org today.

Liguori PUBLICATIONS

Liguori.org • 800-325-9521

Liguori Sacramental Preparation Series

Your Baby's Baptism

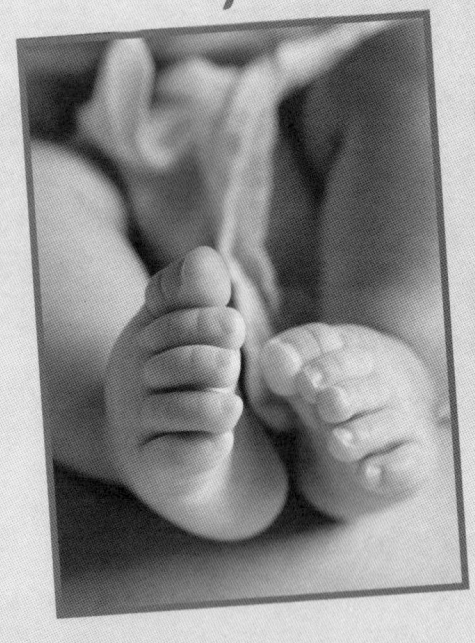

Liguori's best-selling Your Baby's Baptism
Now with Leader Guide — coordinates with the Your Baby's Baptism DVD

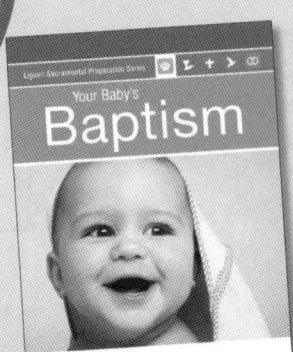

Parent Book
Prepares parents for their baby's special day and reminds them of their own baptismal promises and calling. The parent booklet includes a short history of baptismal practices and traditions, the meaning of the sacrament and its symbols, and a step-by-step guide to the baptismal rite.

16-page booklet
English 825385 • **$4.99**
Spanish 825101 • **$4.99**

Booklets and DVD also available in Spanish

Leader Guide
The wrap-around style of the accompanying *Leader Guide* helps leaders walk parents through the lessons easily. It also includes page-by-page tips for using the Parent Book, a "From the DVD" feature that connects topics to the new **Your Baby's Baptism** video, and even more online!

24-page booklet
English 825392 • **$6.99**
Spanish 825286 • **$6.99**

Companion DVD:

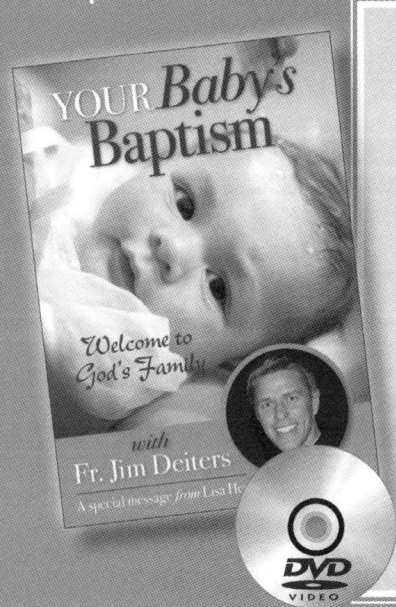

Welcome to God's Family
With Fr. Jim Deiters and a special message from Lisa Hendey

This 30-minute DVD celebrates and renews parents' faith while strengthening their decision to raise their child in the Catholic faith. The DVD covers:
- the importance of baptism for parents and their baby
- an explanation of the stages and symbols of the rite of baptism
- ways to help parents and godparents understand their roles in the spiritual upbringing of the child
- the most commonly asked questions concerning baptism

Special Feature A 7-minute message from Lisa Hendey, creator of *CatholicMom.com* and the *Catholic Mom Moments* blog and podcast, who explains the importance of parents as first teachers of the faith.

30 minutes
English 821943 • **$36.99**
Spanish 822056 • **$36.99**

Visit Liguori.org/baptism for tips on how to get the most from the *Your Baby's Baptism* parent book and companion DVD, and to download the free resources for parents and families, godparents, and parishes.